A Pocket Guide to
How to Start a Successful Group Home

By Yalonda S. Smith

DEDICATION

This book is dedicated to my children, Antonio, Faith, Cierra, and Shantay. Thank you for your unconditional love, support, and understanding when I am too tired to function. Thank you Antonio for taking care of your sisters while I work hard to make our dreams a reality. May God bless each and every one of you to follow your dreams and God's perfect plan for your lives.

CONTENTS

Acknowledgments   i

1   Research   1

2   Licensing Application   8
3   Orientation Class   10
4   Knowing Your Limitations   12
5   Before Purchase or Lease of a Home/Facility   15
6   Physical Site Preparation   19
7   Submit Application Packet   22
8   Compliance Letter   24
9   Final Site Inspection   26
10   Congratulations!!!   27

ACKNOWLEDGMENTS

I would like to first and foremost acknowledgment my father, Jehovah and my Lord and Savior, Jesus Christ. Thank you for the gifts and talents you decided to bless me with. Thank you for making a way out of no way, thank you for choosing me to help make others dreams come true. Thank you to my mother, Margaret Smith, brothers Michael and Frankie, my sisters Mayomi and Dominique, for all your love and support and having my back on this journey. I love you all to life. And last but not least, thank you Almalik for always being there when I need you with love and support.

I also want to say thank you to all my clients who trusted me to be a part of their journey in opening their group home. Each of you helped me to become better at what I do, especially my Texas and Georgia clients! LOL. Many of you have become lifelong friends. That brings me to my sister in Christ and best friend, Harvena Marie who I met through my website. I have only known you about 2 years but it feels like 10! LOL. I want to say thank you for all the times you prayed with me and for me and for all the love and support and for pushing me forward when I wanted to give up. I thank God for bringing you into my life. I pray that all of your dreams and visions come to pass. I love you sis.

1 RESEARCH

Congratulations on your decision to follow your dreams! I know this is a very daunting task and it looks like an overwhelming and scary road ahead. However, that is why I am here! I remember that I was once in your place feeling the same way that you feel right now. I remember feeling excited and scared and nervous and happy all at the same time! I remember when I first made the decision to start my own group home, I searched the internet high and low and could not find any help. Then I finally found one website that offered help for policy and procedure manuals but the prices were through the roof and there was no phone number to get a live customer service representative on the line. You had to order the packet in faith that the website was legitimate and that you weren't throwing your money down the toilet! Call me chicken but I chose not to take that chance!

I remember calling the state licensing department for assistance through the process and I remember them telling me we will send you an application packet. I remember getting this large overwhelming email with the application packet and the state regulations governing group homes. I had no clue what I was doing or what I was looking at. The licensing specialist that was assigned to me explained that I needed to create operating policies and procedures from the state regulations. He also said that these policies and procedures had to be turned in with my application. Then, in an effort to help me, my assigned licensing specialist gave me the number of two other local group home owners so that I can ask them questions to help me get through this process.

I called each group home owner in excitement thinking I can get all my questions answered and maybe get a little bit of guidance from them, but it was an epic disappointment! Neither of them wanted to help me, they wouldn't give me the time of day! They saw me as competition so they gave me these one-word answers to rush me off the phone. Does this sound familiar?

I have had so many clients to tell me that they personally know someone who has a group home such as a family member or old childhood friend, and even THEY would not help them! I finally got referred to another group home owner that was approximately an hour and a half away from me, who at least talked to me; and I think he only help me because I was no competition for him because I was so far away and he had a boys' home and I was opening a girls' home. LOL. He did however, give me some valuable information. He told me how to complete the 6-month start-up budget required by the state of Florida. He also gave me a general overview of the day to day operations of a group home. Lastly, I asked him about the policies and procedures that are required for licensing. I asked if I could purchase a copy of his policies to save some time. I asked him how much would he charge me. He said he had to consult with his board of directors and then came back and told me he will give me a copy of his operating manual for $3,000. I said, $3,000?! Wow! Just for ONE manual?! I said, no thank you, I will try to create the policies myself.

I had a partner at the time and I also worked as a case manager in the foster care system. So I was blessed to have a few individuals in the industry that gave me sample operation forms and my boss at the time gave me a template for a personnel handbook. However, for the operating manual, there was no help! Our first feeble attempt at creating the manual got completely rejected! LOL. The licensing specialist said we basically copied and pasted the state regulations, rather than creating individual policies from the regulations. After a little guidance and explanation of what he was looking for, we managed to submit a manual that passed the second time around. It's funny however, that after 7 years of creating operating manuals, when I looked back at that first manual I laughed and wondered how in the world we ever passed licensing with that manual! It had to be the grace of God because it would never pass in this day in age. It was very basic and bare minimum, but this started my journey to starting a successful group home.

Therefore, I am writing this book because once I got through this process I said to myself that as God has blessed me, I will bless others and because no group home owners wanted to help me when I needed it, I wanted to help those who came after me. I have been doing just that since 2006. I helped everyone the state sent my way to ask me questions and pick my brain. I did it for free back then. LOL. It wasn't until I asked God for other opportunities for growth and expansion that God gave me the idea to turn it into a business when someone asked me could they purchase a copy of my policies so they could cut through the red tape and get through the licensing process as soon as possible.

In Florida, they would tell you that it could take up to one year to get through the licensing process but this was mainly because they knew the polices would be rejected one or twice. After that first sale of a copy of my policies that I actually did customize and change to fit his program, "How to Start a Successful Group Home, LLC" was born, but I did not formally incorporate until 2009.

Now that you know how I began my journey, the first thing you need to do is research the need for group homes in your area. You can do this by going to your state website rather it is the state of Florida, Texas, Virginia, Georgia, etc. Whichever state you live in or want to open a home in has a group home or residential child care licensing department (see **Appendix A** in the back of the book for state listings and websites). Go to your state website and click inside the search box and type licensing for residential child care or residential group homes. Different states use different terminology. For example, the state of Texas group homes are called general residential operations. In Texas, if you say group homes they will think you're talking about foster care group homes which is group homes that you will do in your own home and you would basically be a foster parent but classified as a group home so that you can care for 7 to 12 children. In Texas, general residential operations must have 13 beds at a minimum.

In the state of Florida, they are called group homes. You would either open a small group home or large group home. A small group home is a group home with up to six beds. If you want a home with more than six beds it would be considered a large group home.

When you go to your states website you will see when you type in "licensing" that the state normally licenses two entities, and that is day care centers and group homes. Day care centers may also be done in the home so they may be called day care homes which some people get the applications confused with group homes. So when you are looking at the applications make sure it says licensing application for "residential" group homes or "residential" child caring facilities. "Residential" means the children will be living in the facility versus a day care center or day care home in which children are just there for a certain amount of time. In the state of Georgia, they are called residential child caring facilities instead of group homes.

You want to find the telephone number for the licensing department and call them to ask is there a need for group homes at this time. If you want to service a particular group of clientele such as boys, girls, pregnant teens, etc., ask about the need for that particular group. If there is no need for the particular group of clients you want, ask them what is THEIR need! Needs can fluctuate from month to month in some states.

You must have patience when it comes to contacting the state. It may take you 3 to 5 days just to get a live person on the line. You may have to leave a few voicemails on a few different extensions before receiving a call back and speaking to a live person.

Once you have someone on the line you want to ask all the

questions that you can. Your number one goal is to make sure there is a need in the county or parish or city that you want to put your group home in. Next, you want to ask about contracting. Ask them can they give you the name or contact information of the child placing agencies for the area. This is to speak directly to the organization that will be placing the clients in your home. This is a crucial piece of the research. Without clients, all of this will be for nothing. Once you know that there is a need in your county then you can proceed to ask how to get the application packet for licensing. This step applies to any type of group home that must be licensed by the state, adults with disabilities, foster care, veterans, medically needy, etc.

However, if you are told that they are not accepting applications at this time, do not be discouraged, every county in every state has their own licensing department with a different set of needs.

For example, when I was researching, I lived in Seminole County, Florida. I called the licensing department in my home town and asked the child placing agency if there was a need in my county and they said, "NO". Did I mention that I worked for the child placing agency at the time and knew that the need was great even though they told me no?

You may be like I was and work in the field or have been a foster parent for many years and know there is a desperate need for placements in your area first hand, but they still tell you "NO," there is no need for new group homes". They may say the same thing to you that they said to me 10 years ago! "We are getting away from placing kids in group homes but you can look into becoming a foster parent!" Please know that this is a money issue. ALL states are trying to recruit foster parents and child placing agencies who can then in return recruit foster parents for teens in care because foster parents get paid about 50-75% less than a group home for the same client. I go further into rates later on. My point is that I do not want you to get discouraged. Just know that no matter how much they want to do away with group homes, they simply

CAN'T as long as there are bad, abusive and neglectful parents walking the earth, unfortunately.

So with all that being said, if you get an initial "NO" from the first county that you wanted to have the home in, then check the neighboring counties for need. I called 5 different surrounding counties before I got a "YES'. What if I had given up after 3 calls? We sometimes question God's calling when things do not go as smoothly as we thought it should go as we strive to walk in that purpose. Believe me, this obstacle is just the first of many, so you have to make up in your mind that if God said it, he going to bring it to pass. You must keep a "I will not give up no matter what!" mentality and attitude. However, we cannot be a bystander in the process! When I made that 5th call, I was calling a county two hours away from my home town! Nonetheless, their response was, "When do you plan to open? We place about 300 kids a month! We need placements!" Long story short, I took a leap of faith and made the sacrifice to move two hours away from my home town to follow my dreams and walk in my purpose. I was a single parent of two kids, one of which was a newborn. So if I can do it, so can you…. you just have to decide if it is worth it and if it is God's will for you to make that move.

Now in some states, like Mississippi, they only open up the application process for new group home providers once per year. So in cases such as this, you can get all of your documents together throughout the year and be prepared when they start back accepting applications.

States such as Georgia and Texas may license group homes all year long but only have certain times of year where they give new contracts for the placement of children to new providers. Please make sure you get the deadlines for the contracts. They are normally listed on the state's website in the same place that you can find the license application.

The number one mistake that people make when embarking on this journey is running out and buying or renting a house before they have even completed any research on the need in the area. THAT IS THE WORST AND MOST

EXPENSIVE MISTAKE EVER!! So many people have called me for help AFTER they have already purchased or leased a house. They all say pretty much the same thing. "I saw a house and fell in love with it....it was so perfect for what I wanted to do! I just did not know all the paperwork that was required in this licensing process. No one ever told me all that. Now I have been paying the rent or mortgage on this home for months and I am losing money or almost out of money. No one told me I had to make up policies and procedures!"

Unfortunately, a few of those people ran out of money before they got through the licensing process because they secured the home months in advance of finding my business on the internet. So they sat stuck in the mud, in the middle of the licensing process, not able to move forward because they thought the home was the most important thing.

The state wants to see your policies and procedures and sometimes even a business proposal before even looking at your home. Some states like Virginia (which I love) explicitly tells you NOT to go out and secure a home until the application packet has been approved. Now for the states that want everything all at once, paperwork and proof that you have secured the home as well, I advise you to get the application checklist and get all proper documentation before turning in application. (I will get more in to the required documents in chapter 2). The clock normally starts once you turn in the actual application. Most states give you 30 days to turn in all remaining documents required including proof of home so do not turn in the application until you have everything else on the checklist.

As a recap, please do not lease or purchase a home until you first, have confirmed from licensing and/or the child placing agency that there is a need for new group homes in the area. Next, make sure you have all of your required attachments (everything on the state checklist) for the application to submit to licensing, most importantly the required policies and procedures manuals because they take the most time to create. Rather you are doing the policies yourself, hiring a local consultant, or purchasing this service from my website, take your time to avoid costly mistakes and pitfalls.

2 LICENSING APPLICATION

Some states have the application packets online and some states you have to call and request an application packet. If you cannot find the application it-self online, look for a telephone number for the licensing department and call them and request an application packet. For instance, the states of Georgia and Texas, they have the application packets online but for the state of Florida, you have to call and request an application packet to be emailed to you.

Once you get the application packet you want to do your research on the child placing agency. The licensing department is not the child placing agency in most cases. The licensing department can however give you the name of the child placing agency that you will be contracting with to receive referrals. Again, some states will have all of this information on their state website and some states you will have to just call the phone number to   request the information. Also, do not be alarmed if you speak to a licensing specialist and ask about contracting, and they tell you, you will get that particular information once you get through the licensing process. This was told to a client of mine in Kentucky. As long as licensing has confirmed that the contracting agency is accepting new providers and they make you aware of any deadlines on the contracts, this is okay.

Once you receive the application packet, look through it thoroughly and either on the first page or the last page it will tell you all of the required attachments that are needed when you turn in the application. You cannot just turn the application in by itself. I have written policies and procedures for numerous states throughout the USA and I can tell you that basically they want the same information attached plus or minus a few documents (**see Appendix B for general checklist**). The application packet will ask for attachments such as articles of incorporation, certificate of occupancy, 3 to 6 months' proof of startup capital including a 3-6-month budget to match, an operating manual, personnel policies handbook, operation forms, and a 12-month sample annual budget which shows how you will manage the states funds for the first year that you are in business. Some states such as Virginia and Florida, will also asked for a business proposal of services, business plan, or program statement, before they even allow you to start the application process.

3 STATE ORIENTATION CLASS

Another part of the research phase is attending the state orientation if required by your particular state. The state of Texas and the state of Georgia has group home orientation classes on a monthly basis and you must attend an orientation before you can start the application process. This orientation gives you a brief overview of the licensing process and it allows you to ask questions directly to the licensing department, so utilize this opportunity to get all your questions answered. While you are in the orientation there are a couple of questions you should ask that are very, very, important. Number one, ask how to go about getting contracts for the placement of kids in your home and at what point do you make contact with the contractor. Number two, where do you find the information for the pay rate because in order to do the annual 12-month budget you will need to know the pay rates for your state.

Some states have a set rate that they pay all providers, depending on the level of care needed by the child. Other states allow you to come up with your own rate but it must be comparable to other homes in the area. Pay rates for residential foster care group homes can rage anywhere from $96-$240 per child per day. The rate depends on the level of care needed for the child and the state you are opening the home in. Some states pay a significantly higher rate than others. For example, in Florida, you create your own rate but it must be comparable to other providers in the area. Florida rates for a standard, non-therapeutic group home for teenagers average from $105-$130 per child, per day, depending on what county you open the home in. To give you an example of monthly gross pay for a 6 bed group home, consider the rate of $100 per child per day for a 6 bed home. That would be an average of $3,000 per month, per child, for a total of $18,000 per month if all 6 beds are full every month.

For states such as Texas, the rates are set and the average rate for a general residential operation (known as GRO), the rate is currently $146 per day, per child and you must have a capacity for at least 13 children. This brings in a gross of $56,940 per month for a 30-day period with a full house of 13 children. Now the money is okay in some states and great in others but please keep in mind that this is not a field you get into simply for the money. These vulnerable populations need people who truly care and want to make a difference in their lives.

With all that being said, orientation also serves another purpose. It is also used to weed out all of the people who are not serious about wanting a group home or who may be trying to open a group home for the wrong reason such as money. I have had so many clients call me after an orientation class saying they think they may be in over their head, this is too overwhelming, they not sure if they can do this! However, as I said earlier, this is where professional consulting services may be needed. Whatever you do, do not make an emotional decision to abandon your dreams because you got an overwhelming amount of information in the orientation! I really think they try to scare people in those classes because about half of the people that attend orientation do not continue to pursue the licensing process. So if you're serious about opening up a group home and this is your lifelong dream or you feel like this is your calling, do not give up!

4 KNOWING YOUR LIMITATIONS

Reviewing the application packet can be very overwhelming for most individuals, no matter how book smart or business savvy you maybe. The state regulations are the document in the licensing application packet that typically causes the most stress to applicants or make them feel like they are in over their heads. The state regulations can be from 42 pages to 300 pages long, depending on the state. The state regulations are the state laws governing group homes. These state laws are what you must create your operating manual and personnel policies from. These state laws are like your second Bible. You must learn them and know them like the back of your hand. As I told you in chapter 2, some of the required documents that must be attached to your application will be your operating manual, personnel policies handbook, and all the forms that you will use to operate your group home. For example, you must have admission procedures, service planning procedures, and discharge procedures within your operating manual. You will need forms such as an admission packet, a discharge summary form, incident report form, and a service plan form. The states have a select few forms that you can download from their website such as an incident report form, but that is about all they will give you. The state of Georgia is the only state that

I can remember that will give you a service plan template to use. Other than that you are on your own. There is no state that gives you an operating manual template or a personnel handbook template. You are expected to create these manuals on your own according to your state regulations governing group homes. You cannot pass the licensing process without these manuals.

You must decide what you can do and what you cannot do at this point. You must know your limitations! If you live in a state where a proposal must precede the licensing application packet, you must decide if you are capable of writing this on your own or if you need to hire a professional consultant to write your proposal or business plan or program statement (the name varies by state) for you.

For states that require proposals or program statements such as Virginia and Florida, I found that some clients can write their own proposal and just need help with policies and procedures and some clients may have the capability to do it all but just do not have the time because of work, family, school and other demanding responsibilities.

Whatever you can do, do it. Whatever you cannot do, go to my website at www.helpingdreamscometrue.com and review the different packages I provide on my website. Click on the tab on the right-hand side for how to start a successful group home. For instance, you may be able to write your own proposal of services because you may have experience in this area. However, you may need me to create your operating manual and personnel handbook and all the forms that it takes to operate your home. Or you may need me to complete all of the paperwork for you including your proposal, articles of incorporation, policies and procedures, and operation forms. I have a package called the "ONE STOP SHOP" package that includes everything from beginning to end. This package can even be customized to fit your needs. Some clients come to me who already have incorporated the name of their business through their state which is called articles of incorporation or articles of organization if you are a limited liability company. If you do not know what I am talking about then you need my help! You may say I just would like to do one piece at a time. In that case, you may go on my website and just order the proposal of services first. Once the proposal of services is completed, you submit it to the state licensing department. Once it is reviewed and approved, then you will move on to step two which is the application packet. At this point you will purchase the policies and procedures packet so that I can create your policies procedures and operation forms, everything that you need to operate your group home and pass the licensing process. The policies and procedures normally take me anywhere from 30 to 60 days to complete, depending on how many orders are ahead of you.

This packet also includes budget templates such as your startup budget template, which is either a three month or six-month budget template depending on the state you live in and a 12-month annual budget template that you will use for the application packet and continue to use every year to operate your home. The 12-month budget shows projected income and expenses for the upcoming fiscal year.

Once your paperwork is completed and you have all the documents needed for your application packet you will then need to start looking at homes or facilities to rent or purchase, depending on your financial capabilities. Once you have obtained the facility, you need to think about getting your employees trained if you already have staff identified. Direct care training is also a part of the one-stop shop package or you can purchase it as an individual product when you get to that point. I provide a 3 day, 25-hour training to clients that includes behavior management techniques and training on your operating manual and operation forms that I created for you during the licensing process. All states require your direct care staff to have from 13 to 40 hours of professional training before they can work directly with the children. Each state has a different number of hours required. You may also research local trainings in your area. The state application packet should have a list of relevant topics for trainings.

5 BEFORE PURCHASE OR LEASE OF A HOME/FACILITY

As I said earlier, PLEASE DO NOT PURCHASE OR LEASE A HOME OR FACILITY BEFORE GETTING YOUR POLICIES AND PROCEDURES CREATED!! Yes, I am screaming this at you guys to the top of my lungs!

You have no idea how many clients have come to me after they've already leased or purchased a home because everyone thinks this is the only thing to do to qualify them to open a group home. Some think that if they get a pretty house with pretty furniture and fill out the application to get the license, that is all that it takes, but I am sorry, that is not the case! Paperwork, paperwork, paperwork is the most important thing, that is your priority! I have had too many clients who could not even complete the licensing process due to running out of money in the middle of the licensing process. Why, you ask? It is a very simple thing that people fail to do. Research, research, research, as I stated in chapter one. You cannot go by word of mouth on how to open a group home. You must get the state application packet with the checklist of everything that will be required of you BEFORE running out to purchase or lease a home. This checklist is extensive, and when you get it AFTER you have already purchased the home, you are in for a rude awakening. This is where the licensing process is dragged out much further than they expected because applicants then see that so many documents must be submitted with the application and they must have a qualified program director to manage the group home.

At this point, they are paying rent/mortgage on an empty house for months as they try to create their own policies and procedures or scramble to find someone to help them create them. Unfortunately, many applicants did not anticipate the process lasting so long when they purchased/rented the home and they run out of money and could not afford to keep the property.

I had a client to pay rent on an empty house for eight months before she met me because she had no clue that policies and procedures were required for a home, this was a Florida client. I also had a Georgia client who had a home for about six months before she stumbled upon my website and purchased my policies and her process still took about 12 to 18 months to complete. Every state has a different timeframe. Some states you can get a license in as little as 4 to 6 months while other states it can take from an average of 12 to 15 months. However, do not be discouraged because no matter what the length of time, when purchasing my package, you can cut that time in half. If they tell you it will take up to 12 months to get your home opened, with my help that process will be approximately six months. They quote you so much time because they assume you are creating your own policies and procedures and they know that they will be rejected two or three times before being accepted. However, there is a difference between completely rejected and corrections requested. I will explain this process in chapter 8.

Once you find a house that you like to rent, be sure to inform the landlord of the intended use before signing the lease. The worst thing you could do is lie and tell them it's for personal use and then six months after opening your group home they find out it's a group home and they evict you. If you are using your own personal property, the zoning process is the most important task for you.

The next thing you do once the landlord approves the use, is call your local zoning office and make sure that the home is zoned for a group home. This is the next step for those who already own the property as well. When you give them a call they will ask for the address of the home you want to use and they will run the address and let you know if it can be used for a group home. They will ask you how many clients do you want to take in and what type of clients, rather it is for adults, foster care children, or persons with disabilities.

If zoning gives you the go ahead and tell you that the home is approved for a group home, then I would advise you to call the local fire marshal office and tell them you need to get a pre-inspection or pre-fire inspection on the property to make sure that it is equipped to pass the fire inspection for group homes.

However, if the zoning department tells you that the home is not zoned for a group home and offer you an appeal process or an application to get the home re-zoned, I personally would advise you to find another home. The appeals process and the rezoning process can be a nightmare! However, maybe you have a contact in the zoning office or maybe your zoning officials told you that the process is easy and you have a great chance of getting the house re-zoned, in that case I say proceed with caution. If you plan to purchase this home, do not purchase this home for the sole purpose of a group home without having a final zoning approval! If this home was already your personal property, maybe going through the re-zoning process is worth the challenge.

For fire inspections, if the home failed the pre-inspection of the fire marshal, no worries he will tell you what you need to do to get the facility up to par. Some states require a pull down fire alarm system which can cost anywhere from $3,000 to $7,000. Some states, such as Texas may require a sprinkler system which can cost you up to $10,000 if your home is within the city limits. In some rural areas, however, sprinklers are not required. In states such as Florida, if it is a five bed group home, you will not need a pull down fire alarm system or a sprinkler system. However, if you open a six bed group home you will need a pull down fire alarm system. Many clients have started with a five bed home just to avoid the cost of purchasing the pull down fire alarm system.

All states require you to have fire extinguishers on every floor of the home and they must be commercial grade not the small ones for regular homes. They also must be tested and serviced annually.

The next thing you need to check for is bedroom space. If you hire me as a consultant or you hire another consultant, they will help you to check the state regulations to see what is the square footage requirements for the bedrooms. This is very, very, important because it will tell you how many kids or how many clients you can take into your home. For instance, in the state of Florida there must be 50 ft.^{2} of space for every one child in a bedroom. So if you have a bed room that is 10x10 or 100 ft.^{2} of space you may only have two children in that room. If you have a bedroom that is only 120 ft.^{2} of space and you would like to put three children in that room, you cannot do so. The bedroom must be at least 150 ft.^{2} of space in order to properly placed three children in that bedroom.

Therefore, make sure that the home you select to purchase or rent, has enough bedroom space and living space to accommodate the number of youth you would like to place in your home. Make sure to check the "physical site" section of the state regulations to see what is required in the physical facility as a whole before signing your name on the dotted line of a lease or purchase agreement.

You also need to make sure that you have at least 90 days' worth of working capital to cover the rent until your license is obtained and the contract is in place to receive clients. For example, if the rent is $1,000 per month, make sure you have at least $3,000 in the bank or on credit to cover the rent as you go through the licensing process. Otherwise, this will be a very stressful and long process. Remember, proof of start-up funds documentation will be required with your licensing application packet. Refer to your license application to see if you must show 90 days or 6 months' worth of reserved funds. In Florida and Georgia, it is 6-months of reserved funds required. Most other states only require 3-months.

Last but not least, check to see if your policies and procedures packet and all other documentation is ready to submit to licensing before signing your name on the dotted line of a lease or prior to purchasing a home.

6 PHYSICAL SITE PREPARATION

For your physical site preparation, you should check the state application packet for a physical site checklist. Most states do give you a checklist to make sure that everything is in place. For instance, Arizona, Florida, Ohio, and Kentucky all give you physical site checklists for compliance. I am listing the main things that you need to make sure it is in place for physical site preparation but this should never substitute for your states checklist. The most important pieces to a physical site preparation are your inspections. Most states require you to have a health inspection, fire inspection, and the final inspection by the state licensing specialist.

For your health inspections, they will be looking at things such as: are your chemicals locked up in a closet and inaccessible to your clients? They will ensure that you have running hot water and that your windows have screens in them, that your food is properly stored in the pantry and in the refrigerator. They will also check to make sure that the home is clean and sanitary. They also look at small things like you should have thermometers to make sure that the temperature is right in the freezer and the refrigerator. They will make sure that your medication is in a locked cabinet and inaccessible to clients and they may ask you how will you store leftover food.

For leftovers, for example you must have food storage containers that must be labeled with markers or labeled with a 3-day expiration date so that the clients will not eat one-week old spoiled food.

The fire marshal of course will make sure that there are no electrical wiring issues. The fire marshal will make sure that you have a fire extinguisher on every floor. If a fire alarm system or sprinkler system is required, he or she will make sure that you have the required system and that it was properly installed. He or she will want to see a copy of your blank fire drill log form, which is a part of my forms package. He or she will also make sure that there are no fire hazards in the home or around the property of the group home.

As each inspector give you an inspection report with their signature on it, the report will say whether the home passed or failed the inspection or if you pass pending a few corrections.

They will tell you what you need to do to bring your facility up to par and will have a date to re-inspect your property which will probably be one week or two weeks away. Once you get your final inspection approvals, these inspection reports will become a part of your application packet for licensing.

Next, you can have fun shopping for your beautiful home-like furniture and decor and decorate the home as if you would be decorating for yourself or your loved ones. You want the home to be warm and inviting. That means wall pictures and plants rather live or fake, comfortable furniture, and nicely decorated bed rooms appropriate to the age and gender of your clients.

Once the furniture is in place then you want to work on your office. Make sure you have either two small metal file cabinet or one large 4 to 5 drawer locked file cabinet. You can get these file cabinets from Walmart or OfficeMax, or any office supply store as long as they have a lock with keys.

For your site inspection they will want to see all of your personnel files for each employee and you can look at the operating manual or state regulations to see what should go into the personnel files. They will also want to see at least one mock client file. Again, you can look at your operating manual or state regulations to see what goes into the client files. Next, they want to see your medication cabinet. You will need a small, two drawer file cabinet to store your medication in which you can get from Walmart or Target.

Another thing you should do is print your state regulations out and put them into a three ring binder and put them on the bookshelf in your office. You should always be able to readily refer to your state regulations. In my group home, I put my state regulations in the same binder as my operating manual since the two work hand in hand.

Throughout this preparation process be sure to stay in contact with your licensing specialist and consultant if you decided to work with one. You want to build a rapport with both, but especially your licensing specialist. You want them to know your name whenever you call them.

7 SUBMIT APPLICATION PACKET

Whew!! You finally made it through all of the groundwork and you are ready to submit your application packet! You have your policies and procedures complete, you have all of your forms, you have your articles of incorporation or articles of organization, you have your tax ID number, and last but not least you have your physical site completely prepared for your state inspection!

At this point, I always advise my clients to make an appointment with me to review their application checklist to make sure that every single document that is required is attached. We go through the checklist one by one together. Two eyes are always better than one! If you are doing this on your own without a consultant that is okay, just get your state checklist or application checklist and make a copy of it so that you may write on it, highlight, or mark through each item as you check it off. Your policies and procedures and forms should be in a three ring binder with dividers and each section should be labeled. If your state requires electronic submission you should have electronic folders labeling policy and procedures, operation forms, articles of incorporation, and tax ID documentation. Follow the application instructions for electronic submission and labeling. So either way it should be very organized. Everything should be typed if possible, not handwritten. Review the checklist at least twice! Now submit application.

8 COMPLIANCE LETTER

At this point you have submitted your complete application including all documents and forms according to the application checklist. Now is the waiting game. They will tell you it will take them anywhere from 30 days to 120 days to complete your application review and send you out a compliance letter. Each state may call the compliance letter something different, but at the end of the day they will send you a letter or email stating any errors found in your application packet. Now understand that your packet may be totally rejected or just sent back with specific errors that need to be corrected. Normally, if your policies and procedures are not written correctly, the entire packet can be rejected. On the other hand, the licensing specialist will review them line by line and tell you exactly what policy needs to be corrected and what is missing. Most states have a standard template that they use to inspect your policies and procedures.

They will then give you 30 days to complete those errors and return the corrected information back to them. Do not panic when you receive the compliance letter and it is 2-7 pages long! This is typical. No matter how perfect your application packet may seem, there will always be some corrections needed. That is just the way it goes.

Now here is the beauty of having professional help. Whatever documents were created by your consultant, whether it is myself or another professional, your consultant is responsible for any necessary corrections to those documents including the policies, procedures and forms. You are only responsible for the corrections to documents that you completed, such as the application itself, background check information, employee training information, physical site corrections, etc. However, if you took a stab at completing the policy and procedure manuals yourself and they got rejected, you might want to enlist some help at this point. On the other hand, if they just sent you a correction letter on the policies you created, congratulations! Do not be discouraged by the compliance letter, you did great so give yourself a pat on the back! Just complete the corrections one page at a time or one page per day so it is not so overwhelming.

They will also give you feedback on your budget. They will be reviewing your startup budget and your 12-month budget. If it seems unrealistic to them they will give you suggestions on how to correct it. Once all of your corrections are complete and approved, they will schedule your final site inspection and walk through! Whew! You are almost at the finish line.

9 FINAL SITE INSPECTION

Finally, all of the documents in the application packet has been approved! At this point everything in the house should be in place. The furniture, the fire extinguisher, the fire alarm, and sprinkler system, if required. You should have used your state regulations "physical site" section to make sure that you have everything in place for the final inspection. As I said in the last chapter, once all of your paperwork is approved, they will come out and do this final walk-through. This should actually be a cake walk! When they come out, you should have in a binder, your fire inspection, health inspection, zoning approval letter (if required), and any other inspections that are required. Arizona also has a life safety inspection that is required, so have all of these inspections in one binder or folder ready for the licensing specialist before they can even ask for them.

They will walk through each room of the home making sure it meets state specifications, which this should be no problem if you followed my advice and used the state regulations to properly prepare. Once your state inspection is complete, if there are any compliance issues they will give you up to 30 days to fix those errors and to bring those areas in compliance. Finally, they will come back out and do another walk-through.

Once your physical site has been approved with no errors the state licensing specialist will issue you your license!

10 CONGRATULATIONS!!!

CONGRATUALTIONS YOU ARE THE PROUD OWNER OF A GROUP HOME!!!! Thank you for allowing me to be a part of this journey…. you can breathe now. LOL.

Please visit my website for Cornerstone Consulting & Coaching, LLC at www.helpingdreamscometrue.com for ongoing consulting services that you may need to help you make this first year a SUCCESSFUL one. For best practice, as a new group home owner, I advise you to invest in a mock audit 90-days after opening to ensure that your Program Director and direct care staff are documenting correctly on progress notes, service plans, discharge summaries, admission packets, etc. Getting the doors open is just half the battle. Now you have to keep it open with caring and hardworking staff, excellent documentation, and by following your operating policies and procedures.

All group homes are required to get an annual audit by the state licensing department of their program every year. During this audit, the state licensing specialist will review the program files, including client files, personnel files, incident reports, client grievances, service plans, medication logs, admission/discharge logs, etc. You even have to prepare program statistics to demonstrate that you are doing for the clients what you said you were going to do in your mission statement and program description.

Let me help you to not only survive your audit but to impress your licensing specialist so much that they refer to you as one of the best in the business! When this happens and you want to grow and expand, they will walk you through the process of opening your second home in half the time of the first! I will come out and complete a mock audit of your files, using your state compliance checklist. I will also give you a corrective action plan, just like the state licensing specialist gives you during the real audit when you are out of compliance. This will allow you to fix those areas and bring them into compliance before the real audit. A mock audit will make you feel a little less anxious about the real thing. The mock audit also includes the completion of your program statistics that demonstrates you are meeting your goals for the program.

So invest in yourself and your business, be sure to continue to get professional consulting services from an expert in the field so that you can continue to be the visionary, growing and multiplying your business according to your dreams for years to come...

APPENDIX A
State Licensing Specialists for Foster Care Group Homes

This is the contact information for the state licensing specialist for each state and territory published on the Child Welfare Information Gateway website. They are in alphabetical order.

Alabama Department of Human Resources
Gloria Derico
50 Ripley Street
Montgomery, Alabama 36130-4000
Phone: (334) 242-1650
Fax: (334) 353-2693
Email: Gloria.Derico@dhr.alabama.gov
http://www.dhr.alabama.gov

Alaska Department of Health and Social Services
Yurii Miller
751 Old Richardson Highway
Suite 300
Fairbanks, Alaska 99701
Phone: (907) 451-5075
Fax: (907) 451-2058
Email: yurii.miller@alaska.gov
http://dhss.alaska.gov/ocs/Pages/fostercare/

Alaska Department of Health and Social Services
Tandra Donahue
695 East Parks Highway
Unit 2
Wasilla, Alaska 99654

Phone: (907) 269-3966
Fax: (907) 269-3901
Email: tandra.donahue@alaska.gov
http://dhss.alaska.gov/ocs/Pages/fostercare/

Arizona's Department of Child Safety
Arianna Robinson
3443 N Central Ave.
15th Floor
Phoenix, Arizona 85012
Phone: (602) 255-2805
Fax: (602) 257-7045
Email: AriannaRobinson@azdes.gov

Arkansas Department of Human Services
Kathy Mackay
2017 East Race Street
Searcy, Arkansas 72143
Phone: (501) 268-2714
Fax: (501) 279-1386
Email: Kathy.mackay@dhs.arkansas.gov

California Department of Social Services
Community Care Licensing
744 P Street, MS 17-17
Sacramento, California 95814
Email: Gary.Palmer@dss.ca.gov
http://ccld.ca.gov/default.htm
(http://ccld.ca.gov/default.htm)

Brenda Barner (Acting)
Community Care Licensing
744 P Street, MS 17-17
Sacramento, CA 95814

I started my web-based consulting business, "How to Start a Successful Group Home, LLC in 2009 to help others get through the licensing process of opening a group home. I maintained my group home and my consulting business simultaneously for about 5 years before I closed my group home in November 2013, when the need for group homes declined in my area. At that point in my life I recognized that I enjoyed the consulting more than the day-to-day operations of group home management. I also decided I was ready for a change in environment and decided to leave Florida to explore opportunities in the northeast areas of New York and Pennsylvania as I had been dreaming about for the past two years.

I then stepped out on faith and decided to take my consulting business to the next level and assist others to make their God given visions and dreams a reality on a full-time basis!

In 2016, as the demand increased, I started providing additional services such as incorporation paperwork, direct care training, small business setup (other than group homes) and the one I am most passionate about in this season, life coaching. I became a Tony Gaskins Jr. certified life coach in April 2016. The celebrity life coach, Tony Gaskins, taught me so much during my training program.

ABOUT THE AUTHOR

My name is Yalonda Smith (formerly Yalonda Hooks) and I currently reside in Philadelphia, PA with my children. I am also currently in graduate school to earn my master's degree in psychology with a specialization in Industrial/Organizational Psychology to enhance my skills in program evaluations and quality improvement processes to service other social service/human service organizations outside of group homes.

I owned a successful group home for foster children for 7 years in Jacksonville, Florida, from 2006-2013. I have been in the social service field for 12 years helping women and children in various shapes and forms working to help others find peace, love, and joy in the midst of their storms. I found that overall, through all the different jobs that I held, my greatest passion was goal planning with the different populations, no matter what field or age group. I thoroughly enjoyed seeing their eyes light up as I asked them what did they want to do in life. I have strived to touch as many lives as possible through providing life coaching, life skills training, spiritual coaching including spiritual development and fulfillment, and most importantly by helping them create an action plan to make their dreams a reality.

11. Proof of education/experience for program director and licensed staff such as licensed social worker/counselor or registered nurse; This may include resumes, copy of bachelor's degree, and criminal background check forms for each employee
12. List of staff including position or title and qualifications
13. Abuse registry check from for the Executive Director and CEO
14. Proof of Liability Insurance
15. Obtain written zoning approval from your local zoning office and submit with application

If your licensing specialist asks you for additional items, just place them in the next section. Use dividers with typed inserts if possible. Type a cover page displaying the name of your group home for the notebook and insert it in the clear pocket of the front of the binder.

***This checklist is just to give you a general idea of what is expected with your application for a group home license. Your state application will come with the actual checklist for your particular state to use for the application process.

APPENDIX B

GENERAL GROUP HOME SETUP CHECKLIST
You should present your documents to the licensing agency in a portfolio or three ring binder unless electronic submittal is required. The binder should be a 2 or 3-inch binder with the clear pocket on the front cover. The following contents should be included in your presentation binder to the licensing agency:

1. Application for license/ fee (if applicable)
2. Copy of Articles of Incorporation or Articles of Organization
3. Copy of the Constitution and bylaws (mostly for nonprofits)
4. Nonprofit application (if applicable)
5. Three-month or 6-month startup budget with proof of reserved funds (varies depending on the state)
6. One year Projected Expenses Budget
7. Organizational Chart
8. List of Officers and governing body w/contact information
   a. State the terms of service for each position of the board
9. Operation Procedures that conforms to state regulations including:
   a. Statement of Purpose/Mission Statement
   b. Objective
   c. Scope of Services provided
   d. Specify targeted youth
10. Admission Packet

Wisconsin Department of Children and Families
Mary Morse, State Licensing Program Specialist
201 East Washington Avenue
PO Box 8916
Madison, Wisconsin 53708
Phone: (262) 548-8694
Fax: (262) 521-5314
Email: Mary.Morse@wisconsin.gov
http://www.dhs.wisconsin.gov/

Wisconsin Department of Health and Family Services
201 East Washington Avenue
Madison, Wisconsin 53703
Phone: (608) 266-8946
Email: emily.tofte@wisconsin.gov
http://www.dhs.wisconsin.gov/
Emily Tofte

Wyoming Department of Family Services
2451 Foothill Boulevard
Suite 103
Rock Springs, Wyoming 82901
Phone: (307) 352-2509
Fax: (307) 352-2560
Dana Ward
Email: **dana.ward@wyo.gov**

**These results are current as of Monday, January 2, 2017 unless otherwise noted on their website. I am not responsible for out dated information.

**In the event that the contact person is no longer working there, just ask for the "licensing department" and inform them you would an application packet to open a residential group home.

Phone: (340) 774-4393
Fax: (340) 774-0082
Cherlyn Bradford

Virginia Department of Social Services
1604 Santa Rosa Road
Suite 130
Richmond, Virginia 23229
Phone: (804) 726-7271
Email: robin.ely@dss.virginia.gov
https://www.dss.virginia.gov/contact_us/dolp_district.

Laura Polk
Department of Social Services
801 East Main Street
Richmond, VA 23219
Email: laura.polk@dss.virginia.gov

Washington Department of Social and Health Services
PO Box 45700
Olympia, Washington 98504
Phone: (360) 902-8349
Email: wrighks@dshs.wa.gov
Kristina Wright

West Virginia Department of Health and Human Resources
350 Capitol Street -- Room 691
Charleston, West Virginia 25301
Phone: (304) 356-4570
Fax: (304) 558-4563
Email: Christina.M.Bertellicoleman@wv.gov
Christina Bertelli Coleman

Texas Department of Family and Protective Services
3635 SE Military Drive
E-550
San Antonio, Texas 78223
Phone: (210) 337-3083
Fax: (512) 934-9647
Email: erika.almanza@dfps.state.tx.us
http://www.dfps.state.tx.us
Erika Almanza

Utah Department of Human Services
Office of Licensing
195 North 1950 West
Salt Lake City, Utah 84116
Phone: (801) 538-4242
Fax: (801) 538-4553
Email: dhsol@utah.gov
http://hslic.utah.gov/

Vermont Department for Children and Families
280 State Drive
Waterbury, VT 05671
Email: James.Forbes@vermont.gov

Jim Forbes
Phone: (802) 241-0887
Email: Jim.Forbes@vermont.gov

Virgin Islands Department of Human Services
1303 Hospital Ground
Building A-Knud Hansen Complex
St. Thomas, VI 00802

Rhode Island Department of Children, Youth, and Families
Kevin Savage
101 Friendship Street, 4th Floor
Providence, Rhode Island 02903
Phone: (401) 528-3629
Fax: (401) 528-3666
Email: Kevin.Savage@dcyf.ri.gov
http://www.dcyf.ri.gov/licensing.htm

South Carolina Department of Social Services
PO Box 1520
Columbia, South Carolina 29201
Phone: (803) 898-7511
Email: jacqueline.lowe@dss.sc.gov
http://www.state.sc.us/dss/fosterhome/index.html
Jacqueline Lowe

South Dakota Department of Social Services
Child Protection Services
700 Governor's Drive
Pierre, South Dakota 57501-2291
Phone: (605) 773-3227
Email: Josh.Thorpe@state.sd.us
https://dss.sd.gov/childprotection/licensing.aspx
Josh Thorpe

Tennessee Department of Children's Services
1272 Foster Avenue
Nashville, Tennessee 37210
Phone: (615) 532-5598
Email: Mark.Anderson@tn.gov
http://state.tn.us/youth/
Mark Anderson

Oregon Department of Human Services
Office of Licensing and Regulatory Oversight
500 Summer Street NE, DHS First Floor E-13
Salem, Oregon 97301-1066
Phone: (503) 373-0217
Fax: (503) 378-2558
Email: harry.gilmore@state.or.us
http://www.oregon.gov/dhs/providers-
partners/licensing/Pages/index.aspx
Harry Gilmore

Pennsylvania Department of Human Services
625 Forster Street
Health and Welfare Building, Room 103
Harrisburg, Pennsylvania 17120
Phone: (717) 214-9780
Fax: (717) 214-3784
Ellen Whitesell
Email: ewhitesell@pa.gov

Roseann Perry
11 Stanwix Street
Room 260
Pittsburgh, PA 15222
Phone: (412) 565-5168
Email: rosperry@pa.gov

Puerto Rico Administration for Children and Families
PO Box 11398
San Juan, Puerto Rico 00910-1398
Phone: (787) 294-4900
Email: rrodriguez@familia.pr.gov
Raquel Rodriguez Gauthier

http://www.ncdhhs.gov/providers/licensure/facility-licensure/social-services
Rita Bland

North Dakota Department of Human Services
600 East Boulevard Avenue
State Capitol, Department 325
Bismarck, North Dakota 58505
Phone: (701) 328-4934
Toll-Free: (800) 245-3736
Fax: (701) 328-3538
Email: kmbless@nd.gov
Kelsey Bless

Ohio Department of Job and Family Services
PO Box 183204
Columbus, Ohio 43218-3204
Phone: (330) 252-6574
Fax: (330) 252-6590
Email: Monica.Kress@jfs.ohio.gov
Monica Kress

Oklahoma Department of Human Services
801 Kingsberry Rd
Holdenville, Oklahoma 74848
Phone: (405) 521-3646
Phone: (405) 379-7231
Email: Wendy.Argo@okdhs.org
http://www.okdhs.org
Wendy Argo

Karen Moyer-Shapiro
225 West State Street
Trenton, NJ 08625
Email: Karen.Moyer@dcf.state.nj.us

New Mexico Department of Children, Youth and Families

PERA Building, Room 219
PO Drawer 5160
Santa Fe, New Mexico 87502
Phone: (505) 827-8459
Fax: (505) 476-1023
Email: Yolanda.castro@state.nm.us
Yolanda Castro de Esquibel

New York Office of Children and Family Services

52 Washington Street
Room 332 North
Rensselaer, New York 12144
Phone: (518) 474-9603
Toll-Free: (800) 345-5437
Fax: (518) 486-6326
Email: Susan.Gilman@ocfs.ny.gov
Susan Gilman

North Carolina Department of Health and Human/Division of Social Services

820 S. Boyland Avenue
Dorothea Dix Campus - McBryde Building
Raleigh, North Carolina 27603-2246
Phone: (919) 527-6352
Fax: (919) 715-6714
Email: rita.bland@dhhs.nc.gov

PO Box 94986
301 Centennial Mall South
Lincoln, Nebraska 68509
Phone: (402) 471-6288
Fax: (402) 471-9034
Email: Jodi.Allen@nebraska.gov

Nevada Department of Health and Human Services
4126 Technology Way
3rd Floor
Carson City, Nevada 89706
Phone: (775) 684-4434
Fax: (775) 684-4456
http://dcfs.nv.gov/Programs/CWS/Placement/)

Dorothy Pomin, Foster Care Specialist
Email: dpomin@dcfs.nv.gov

New Hampshire Department of Health and Human Services
Linda Deneau
129 Pleasant Street
Brown Building
Concord, New Hampshire 03301
Phone: (603) 271-4953
Fax: (603) 271-4729
http://www.dhhs.nh.gov/dcyf/adoption/

New Jersey Department of Children and Families
225 West State Street
Trenton, New Jersey 08625
Phone: (609) 826-3882
Email: Karen.Moyer@dcf.state.nj.us

Mississippi Department of Human Services
Division of Family and Children Services
750 North State Street
Jackson, Mississippi 39202

Chandar Turner
Phone: (601) 359-4986
Email: Chandar.Turner@mdhs.ms.gov

Missouri Department of Social Services
205 Jefferson Street
Jefferson City, Missouri 65103
Phone: (573) 522-1191
Fax: (573) 526-3971
Email: Elizabeth.Tattershall@dss.mo.gov
Elizabeth Tattershall

Montana Department of Public Health and Human Services
PO Box 8005
301 S. Park Avenue
Helena, Montana 59604-8005
Phone: (406) 841-2415
Fax: (406) 841-2487
http://www.fostercare.mt.gov

Theresa C. Becker
PO Box 8005
301 S. Park Avenue
Email: tbecker@mt.gov

Nebraska Department of Health and Human Services
Jodi Allen

Massachusetts Department of Early Education and Care
Carmel Sullivan
51 Sleeper Street, 4th Floor
Boston, Massachusetts 02210
http://www.mass.gov/edu/government/departments-
and-boards/department-of-early-education-and-care/
Phone: (617) 988-6631
Fax: (617) 988-2451
Email: carmel.sullivan@state.ma.us

Michigan Department of Human Services
201 North Washington
PO Box 30650
Lansing, Michigan 48909
Email: rehagenc@michigan.gov

Christine Rehagen
Phone: (517) 284-9741
Fax: (517) 284-9727

Minnesota Department of Human Services
Human Services Building
444 Lafayette Road North
St. Paul, Minnesota 55155
Phone: (651) 431-3512
Fax: (651) 431-7673
Email: cory.a.jelinek@state.mn.us
Cory Jelinek

http://www.kdheks.gov/bcclr/foster_care.html
Daric Smith

Kentucky Cabinet for Health and Family Services
275 East Main Street – 3C-E
Frankfort, Kentucky 40621-0001
Phone: (502) 564-7962
Fax: (502) 564-9350
Email: Greg.davidson@ky.gov
http://chfs.ky.gov/os/oig/drcc.htm
Greg Davidson

Maine Department of Health and Human Services
2 Anthony Avenue, SHS #11
Augusta, Maine 04333
Phone: (207) 624-7964
Fax: (207) 287-6156
http://www.maine.gov/dhhs/bcfs/fosteradopt.htm
Linda Brissette
Email: Linda.Brissette@maine.gov

Maryland Department of Human Resources
312 West Saratoga Street
Baltimore, Maryland 21201
Darlene Ham
Phone: (410) 767-7447
Email: darlene.ham@maryland.gov

April Edwards
311 West Saratoga Street
5th Floor, Room 576
Baltimore, Maryland 21201
Phone: (410) 767-7195
Email: april.edwards@maryland.gov

Idaho Department of Health and Welfare
Kelle Johnson
450 West State Street, 5th Floor
Boise, Idaho 83702
Phone: (208) 334-5700
Fax: (208) 332-7330
Email: Johnson2@dhw.idaho.gov

Illinois Department of Children and Family Services
Denice Murray
Division of Foster Care and Permanency Services
406 East Monroe Street
Springfield, Illinois 62701-1498
Phone: (312) 814-2074
Email: Denice.Murray2@illinois.gov

Indiana Department of Child Services
June Artis, Unit Manager
302 West Washington Street
Room E306, MS 08
Indianapolis, Indiana 46204
Phone: (317) 234-4507
Fax: (317) 234-4633
Email: Beverly.Gatling@dcs.in.gov
http://www.in.gov/dcs

Kansas Department of Health and Environment
1000 SW Jackson, Suite 200
Curtis State Office Building
Topeka, Kansas 66612
Phone: (785) 296-0202
Email: info@kdheks.gov

Phone: (302) 892-5800
Fax: (302) 633-5112
Email: occl.dscyf@state.de.us
http://kids.delaware.gov/occl/occl.shtml

Florida Department of Children and Families
Xiomara Turner
1317 Winewood Boulevard
Building 1
Tallahassee, FL 32399-0700
Phone: (850) 717-4659
Fax: (850) 487-0688
Email: Xiomara.turner@myflfamilies.com

Georgia Department of Human Services
Carol Winstead
2 Peachtree Street, NW
Suite 28-232
Atlanta, Georgia 30303
Phone: (404) 657-9611
Fax: (404) 657-5708
Email: cswinste@dhr.state.ga.us

Hawaii Department of Human Services
Tracey Yadao
810 Richards Street
Suite 400
Honolulu, Hawaii 96813
Phone: (808) 586-8257
Fax: (808) 586-4806
http://www.hawaii.gov/dhs

Phone: (916) 651-5335
Fax: (916) 654-1691
Email: Brenda.Barner@dss.ca.gov

Child and Family Services Agency
Valerie Douglas
200 I Street, SE
Child and Family Services Agency
Washington, DC 20003
Phone: (202) 727-2111
Email: valerie.douglas@dc.gov

Colorado Department of Social Services
Nicole Sherwood
Division of Child Care
1575 Sherman Street
Denver, Colorado 80203
Phone: (303) 866-3185
Fax: (303) 866-4359
Email: Nicole.Sharwood@state.co.us

Connecticut Department of Children and Families
Jim McPherson
505 Hudson Street
Hartford, Connecticut 06106
Phone: (860) 550-6532
Fax: (860) 566-6726
Email: jim.mcpherson@ct.gov

Delaware Department of Services for Children, Youth and Their Families
Cynthia Brown
1825 Faulkland Road
Wilmington, Delaware 19805

In providing so many services outside of policies and procedures for group homes, I changed the name of my business to reflect the expansion, Cornerstone Consulting & Coaching, LLC. I love that my business is location-independent and that I can travel the world and still work as long as I have my laptop and internet access. Please email me with any questions about my book or the licensing process at **yalonda@helpingdreamscometrue.com**. Also, check out my website at **www.helpingdreamscometrue.com** to get help with the licensing process or life coaching, to get on an action plan with support, encouragement, and motivation to move forward in life to make your dreams a reality, whatever they may be.

14427178R00035

Made in the USA
Lexington, KY
07 November 2018